Your Wilder Nature

Your Wilder Nature

A FIELD GUIDE TO TRACKING SOUL

Daian Hennington, MSW

MONTEREY, CALIFORNIA

Daian Hennington
PO BOX 813
Monterey, California 93942

www.daianhennington.com

Cover design by TheMagnoliaAgency.com

Original art including cover art by Gerald Webber, Big Sur, CA

Book Layout ©2015 BookDesignTemplates.com

Ordering Information:

Available from Amazon.com and other retail outlets. Special discounts are available on quantity purchases by associations and others. For details, contact the address above.

The material in this book is intended for educational purposes only. No expressed or implied guarantee as to the effects of the use of the recommendations can be given nor liability taken.

Your Wilder Nature: A Field Guide to Tracking Soul/Daian Hennington.

—1st ed.

ISBN-13: 978-0-692-74743-8
ISBN-10: 0-692-74743-5

Dedicated with love to my parents
Benjamin H. Hazard and Sumie C. Hazard

*Forget not that the earth delights to feel your bare feet
and the winds long to play with your hair.*

—KHALIL GIBRAN

*I only went out for a walk and finally concluded to stay out
till sundown, for going out, I found, was really going in.*

—JOHN MUIR

Contents

Acknowledgements

THIS BOOK SHARES A lifetime of lessons from my teachers. I am indebted to all of them for giving of themselves and hope that I have been able to understand their wisdom well enough to summarize for you in this book. Errors and omissions are all mine.

For guidance and support in creating this book I thank my editors Jill Bailin and Katherine Malmo, and for tips and encouragement in the writing process I thank friend and screenwriter Renaldo Primus at Garden Street Productions. For holding me to my commitment to work on my book every single week and providing unflagging encouragement, I am indebted to fellow writer Emily Ann Peterson. I am grateful to Gerald Webber, Big Sur artist, for his beautiful line drawings of spirit animals. A big thank you also to Chandler Bolt, Jaime Grodberg and everyone at the Self-Publishing School for helping me to actually finish this work and get it published. Thank you Cousette Copeland for your writing advice.

I am most grateful to my parents Benjamin and Sumie Hazard who nurtured our multi-cultural polyglot household of students, artists, rebels and adventurers, and who brought my three sisters and I into this world to be hopeful, loving and strong women. Thank you sisters, Alyne and Malyne Hazard and Francesca Custodia. Thank you to the future of the family Ben, Sophia, Collin, Maria, Na'Dra, Na'Auni and Edward.

Thanks also to my parents and family elders who maintained our ties to nature as teacher, medicine, inspiration, and as a spiritual home, and who trusted enough to let me go out and wander California's beautiful wildlands. Much gratitude to my brothers and sisters who tell the stories, keep the ceremonies and honor the elders at Mt. Madonna and Indian Canyon and wherever Spirit is remembered. Thank you, thank you, thank you.

Gratitude also to the School of Lost Borders for being midwife to soul for all people through wilderness rites of passage. Beth Beurkens, poet, guide and teacher, thank you for introducing me to the wilderness rites of passage in your life-changing Woman Quest program. Many thanks to the California Naturalist Program offered by the University of California, and especially as it is taught at the Pacific Grove Museum of Natural History. Thank you to the National Outdoor Leadership School for their excellent Wilderness First Responders training.

I am grateful to friends, colleagues and clients who taught me about service, perseverance and grace during my years as a social worker for the people of the County of Monterey. Thank you Meg, Keri, Brenda and Claudia, my "boots on the ground" social work sisters from the Department of Veterans Affairs, Monterey Clinic homeless program. Thank you to the brothers who had my back in the streets and at encampments serving homeless veterans. Thank you Wayne and Tony. Special thanks to those brave souls who joined me on earth walks, summer day camps and youth rites of passage over the years.

I owe my husband and best friend, Glenn P. Hennington, the most loving gratitude for his patience and patience and patience, and bringing home meals, and supporting me with love, unlimited shoulder rubs, and more patience. I could not do any of this without you.

And with greatest love and gratitude to the Spirit who moves with me and through me and shelters me and who I have known in the mountains and on the sea, in every wood, river and desert, and in the grace of a cougar and the heart of a bear. Thank you, thank you, thank you, thank you.

Introduction

TO FIND OURSELVES IN wild nature is to be in the presence of something greater and more powerful than we can comprehend. Away from human habitation, we enter a place instinctual and free, ruled by the forces of earth, sky, and water. Wild nature is the world as created. Surfers, rock climbers, and mountaineers are acutely aware of the power and presence they move through. It is much more than any of us can immediately see or control. We come to face soul in all its darkness and light. We grapple with fear and transcendence. We are in the presence of the sacred.

It was in the Hetch Hetchy Valley of Yosemite National Park that I first learned about power from Bear and Cougar. On the trail, I was taught about holding boundaries from a mother bear with her cub. From Cougar, I learned about mystery and not to assume that what I think I see is all there is. That was the night a black shape leapt off a boulder and landed silently next to me. I reached for my flashlight but the shape darted away and I could only see eyes glowing back at me from behind a bush. I wondered that a bear could land so lightly; bears were my daily reality. Later, in the light of day, I met that graceful mystery again, and it was Cougar.

I came to this place following in my father's footsteps. He would tell my sisters and me about the month-long horse pack trip he took into the southern Sierra Nevada mountains as a young man. So it was natural in my mind to make my own wilderness rite of passage into adulthood. I was eighteen years old. In the week I spent alone and fasting I learned much about self-reliance and other important lessons of adulthood, and to open my mind to subtle messages from a wilder world.

In that adventure I had set out on a young adult's search for meaning and vision. It was a chaotic time. Every evening, with the rest of America, I had a clear view of the death and destruction of the Vietnam War. The hope and brutality of the Civil Rights Movement was constantly before us as well. Failing social structures fought to hold ground and the social order shifted daily. I write this now and think "same song, different verse."

Today, however, the stakes are higher. Not only is human society in transition, our home planet is, too. So many of us are alienated, from each other, from self, and from the natural world. We experience loneliness and a disconnect in our personal lives. The earth suffers from our careless disregard. It is time to seek a new vision, for ourselves and for the earth. We are called to soulful inquiry and to heal the broken relationships. This book is an invitation to renew the old relationships of mutual care, as it helps guide you through exploring self and soul in nature.

Humans need the natural world. Indeed, the word "human" has roots in common with the word "humus," which is, of course, the earth. Biologist E.O. Wilson wrote in *Biophilia* of humanity's innate love for and attraction to living things as "the connections that human beings subconsciously seek with the rest of life." All my life I've had an affinity for nature and I've been lucky enough to have parents who trusted and encouraged this connection. I began my intimate relationship with the natural world in Berkeley's Wildcat Canyon, where I greeted the live oaks and pines as my companions, and explored the creeks and caves and the spicy shade of laurel trees. In childhood camping experiences I learned that a person could live happily and have plenty of fun without a lot of "stuff."

The lessons I learned in the wild led me to explore the ways of indigenous people, consciousness as experienced across cultures, the pursuit of psyche – both personally and professionally, and led me to an appreciation for the sacred expressed in any form or language. I also learned from my own unusually varied family cultures: Asian, Native, African, and European. My work has been informed by research on the benefits of spending time in nature and studies on complementary health practices. With a master's in social work, I have provided mental health services to children, youth, and families, and I've been honored to serve veterans, and the homeless. I have a love for sharing explorations of self in nature and I offer workshops on the California Central Coast.

Over time I've learned some simple ways of engaging wild soul. Wild soul is "pre-conquest" and calls to us in wide open spaces, in the deep, and in our own animal mystery. It is a song of ourselves, authentic and unfettered, native to the earth. For this I thank the Creator and every helping spirit, my family, friends, and community, and every teacher - human or other than human. All cultures have practices that nurture the development of self and spirit, many of which require dedication or initiation into a traditional path. What I offer is a way of connecting with soul in nature that can be practiced by anyone of any belief, any age, any culture, any physical ability. This book explores a way that has kept us well and allowed us to survive and thrive as individuals and communities for thousands of years. Nature is a powerful teacher.

Your Wilder Nature is not intended as therapy, but it does offer healing. I encourage you to seek the support of a qualified counselor as needed or to consult with your therapist on the activities herein if you are currently in therapy. As in any outdoor or physical activity, there are inherent risks, so please seek the advice of your physician to determine whether such activities are suitable to your situation. The stories herein tell the experiences of real people, but no personally identifiable names or identities are disclosed in this book.

The chapters that follow are a guide for tracking soul in nature. In this book you will learn practices of awareness and observation. You will learn skills of orienting to self and the natural world, tracking, and outdoor safety. As well, you will learn to read the signs and understand the language of psyche and nature. Chapters discuss both ideas that might be termed psychological or spiritual in nature, and at other times offer practical outdoor advice. Using these skills and a dawn-to-dusk walking ceremony called the earth walk, we track the edge of worlds in the border-lands between nature and soul.

We are people who have always known the sacred living presence around us. We find blessing in a sunrise and God on a mountaintop. We talk to our dogs and cats and birds, and we know they understand. In just this way, Sage, Salmon, Bear, and Hawk invite you to a biodiversity of the spirit. In the simplest terms, we come to nature not because scientific research convinces us of the benefits, but because of how we feel in body, mind, and spirit. Your soulful life is more deep, and thrilling and more adventurous than any online game or novel. Find meaning. Find balance. You won't be lost. You will be connected for life.

A Wilder Nature

CHAPTER 1

A Wilder Nature

DOUBLE-BOOKED AND SCREEN-BLINDED; the diagnosis is "burnout," "soul hunger," or "life crisis" and we are lost. Am I burned out? No, more like crispy fried. Do you know this feeling? We try to fill the empty space in our hearts with food, drink, or distraction to the point of addiction. Some of us are trapped in the web of the internet or snared by the quests and visions of a virtual reality that appears to be more vivid than the life in front of us. Doctors tell us that in many cases, our epidemic of chronic and debilitating illnesses, heart and kidney disease, diabetes, hypertension, painful joints, and immune deficiencies can be traced back to how we live.

The answer to the problem is out there, and it's being paraded right in front of us every day. Marketing research exploits the science of desire. Freedom and adventure in majestic Western landscapes beckon in advertisements and ignite a hunger inside. Images of a lightning storm chasing a 4-wheel drive across the high desert, a climber bagging a peak, or a family campfire next to a lake speak to the heart and show us where we long to be. Yet instead of a soulful encounter we are offered a brand new SUV or a granola bar.

How do we find ourselves again? How do we feed the hunger, heal the heart? The answer is in what we do intuitively, naturally, instinctively: we go out for air. We walk on the beach, drive with the windows down, find solace in healing waters, or head for a rooftop and gaze at the stars. Science confirms our intuition by noting the drop in stress hormones and blood pressure following a fifteen-minute walk in the woods. Perhaps we relax in natural surroundings because ultimately, this is where we come from.

Legend has it that there was once a time when the animals knew our speech, and we knew theirs. There was once a time when we knew in our marrow that the same spirit that enlivened the Great Bear ran hot in our blood too. Wherever we were, we knew the land was alive, we were not alone, and we shared a relationship with all living things. Even now, seeing the fire of sunset on the horizon, or stopping the shush of skis to hear the silence of a deep snowfall, we can feel the connection. However, life in the fast lane has cut too many off from this communion. Many are lost.

Earth suffers from our broken relationship as well. The industrial overdraft of rivers and aquifers parches the soil. It causes plants to die, and children drink poisoned water. The tender relationship of care and respect is broken. Thoughtless consumption of resources and the excretion of carbon and chemical waste change weather patterns. The ancient cycle of seasons that set the dance in motion is off-kilter. Pollinators arrive before buds have opened. It is not cold enough to sweeten the maple. Salmon wait offshore to return to their spawning grounds, but the rivers that would carry them home no longer reach the sea. Earth is injured as we are injured from the broken relationship. The dancers are out of step.

On the spring equinox I joined in the worldwide "Bless the Water" day and went to the Salinas River in California, near my home. The river was beautiful, strong-flowing, and wide, but nitrogen run-off from agricultural fields fed algae bloom along its banks. My heart ached as I considered the death of nestlings and marine life from toxic poisoning, and the disregard for plant and animal communities that depend on the river. Yet the rushes and cattails were still abundant, and the river's spirit was strong. I took hope in the knowledge that others around the world were also gathered at water sources that day to recognize that water is sacred. I thanked the river and I felt blessed in return.

These days most of us live far-removed from the immediate knowledge that we rely on the natural world for our survival. Yet a new awareness of our relationship grows daily. We hear news of climate change, and we are directly affected by super-storms, drought, and other unwanted changes to our planet. The physical manifestations of this disconnect are clear and can be seen on the news nightly. The psychic effects of this disconnect are subtler but no less life-disturbing.

In an earlier time, people who lived close to wildness and nature had an intimate relationship with the land. They celebrated their kinship with the natural world and gave thanks for the gifts of life the land provided. These practices continue in cultures that honor the heritage of that natural connection or still live closely with the land. People who gather wild plants for healing and for traditional ceremonies still ask their plant relations for permission to harvest and express their gratitude. The necessity of connection is basic. The umbilicus, and unseen heart connection, bind mother to child. In the best of worlds, we are nourished and protected. Even without such a beginning, we long for that connection. How do we consciously renew that relationship? If the problem is an injured self and an injured planet, the solution lies in healing the injured relationship.

People want to connect with something bigger, something deeper. Nature brings us right up against soul. We long for the meaningful and mysterious. We know when we've found a connection. We hear it in that still, small voice inside. The connection is there when we are inspired and enlarged. It is in hands that create, work, write; in voices that sing and tell stories. It calls to us in dreams. We feel it in the inspired movement of the body and in music. We feel at once enlarged and humbled when after a long hike we stand encircled by high mountain peaks, or at night under the great wheel of circling stars. In the swell and rhythm of the sea, and in the delicate patterns of sand left by the waves, soul speaks to us and we understand.

I like the description of soul as the essential part or fundamental nature of anything. We use the word "soul" to describe authenticity, such as in the case of a person who speaks or sings soulfully. We say a person who has "sold their soul" has lost integrity. We describe the grief of internal conflict as the dark night of the soul. Soul has also been defined as the spiritual part of a being. While a concise definition is just out of reach, we feel it viscerally.

How does one begin to reconnect with self and soul? Asking questions is a good start. At a crossroads, mid-life, wondering how long to hold on to the job? Wondering how the job will feed the spirit as well as the family, and at what cost? We do what we must. Not enough soul food, however, results in burnout and soul hunger. We look for meaning and ask, is this all there is?

Questions come early in life as well as late. A young person wonders if they have chosen the right school, vocation, relationship, and if they have what it takes to make it in the world. Life is full of choices, like so many rabbit trails through the brush. We pose these questions to ourselves, to spiritual advisors, and to our friends. These questions form the foundation of our most important human dialogue. We are called to be in dialogue with soul.

What are you seeking? How will you find it? Trackers know. You begin with the hint of a presence. Follow some bent grass, a depression in the ground, a print on the earth. Track the mystery until you learn how she moves, what she needs, when she rests.

On the wildlands at Fort Ord National Monument one weekend, I track the passage of an unseen being. Markings left in the soft dirt show solid track walls with some depth and soft rounded pads without claw markings. Feline. I kneel to measure, using the ruled edge of my notebook; is that really four inches across? Cougar? I survey the perimeter to see who might be observing me. As an excellent tracker herself, if my unseen friend is still in the vicinity, she is no doubt at a motionless stop. Tracking the edge of the human-wildland interface, a borderland touching both our spheres, I am wildly alive.

Go out onto the land, track this edge of worlds. Begin by building an intimate relationship with one spot; learn the names of the inhabitants. You will come to know who appears at each season, the birthing times, the fledging times, and the dying away times. The relationship becomes personal and you, yourself, will come to be known in that place. The open sky invites you to be in relationship with the cycles of night and day, the returning seasons, the sequence of life, death, and renewal. Renew and strengthen one relationship with the wild, and the world is changed.

We are called to be in relationship with the earth. All of us are descended from people who honored the sacredness of Earth. We are the people of the Sacred Groves and Springs of Europe; the Mayan Ya'axche World Tree that connects all the worlds; the great river spirits of Africa, Nil and Oshun; the Asian nature gods and spirits; the Holy Ganges River; and Mother Earth and Father Sky.

Instinctively, we seek to connect to soul in nature, to communicate, and to make a relationship. We remember that this land is fully alive. That is how our ancestors saw the world, and deep down it remains part of us. How do we begin? We begin by finding our place in the world. We begin by finding our own true north.

Pause for a moment and reflect:

- How do you feel in body, mind and heart at this moment in your life? In what way are you comfortable, in what way are you uncomfortable.

- What is your experience of being in nature? What was it as a child? What is it now?

- What is your relationship with the natural world?

- How do you express your soulful life?

Orienting

CHAPTER 2

✻

Orienting

EXPLORERS AND DEEP-WATER SAILORS navigate the unknown by locating true north. A compass shows magnetic north, which shifts according to the location of magnetic poles and is influenced by the presence of attractive metals or energy fields. True north, on the other hand, is constant and can be determined by the position of the stars in every hemisphere. The star Polaris remains fixed in the north, the constellation of the Southern Cross shows the way in the south, and the Belt of Orion is anchored at the equator.

If we know our own true north, we can create an inner map to help us plot out the course of our lives and cross through unfamiliar or dangerous terrain safely. To find our own true north we must seek out the boundaries, features, and directional signs of our inner landscape. A hundred years ago a person's life would have been clearly mapped out by gender, race, class, culture, and family occupation. Today's world is wider and the choices more abundant. These days, not many of us are apprenticed to our father's trade or our mother's craft. Many influences present themselves. How then, do we plot our own course? We do it by finding our own true north.

To know where we stand right now, we orient ourselves by observing, questioning, and testing. We practice self-awareness. We come to understand physical, emotional, mental, and spiritual aspects of ourselves. Through self-awareness we become attuned to our own directional markers. Here are some tools to help map out our own true north.

Journaling

An explorer, captain, or naturalist keeps a field notebook or log to chronicle daily observations about location, season, habitat, weather, and conditions. A tracker of the inner terrain uses a personal journal to record current conditions, dreams, and realizations.

A journal need not be written. It can include drawings, maps, and symbols. Cut-out pictures pasted in a book are an evocative way to express your thoughts. Pictographs carved in rock, painted murals, and other ancient histories tell stories as well as words on paper. The staff of an African griot records the history of a tribe, and the painted ceiling of the Sistine Chapel in Rome clearly depicts a spiritual journey.

Keeping a personal journal allows us to ask questions and listen to our own thoughts and feelings freely. An old-fashioned physical notebook is your companion in the field. It is your friend in exploration at all hours. It can serve as a guide through the dark and help you retrace your steps to where you began.

To start, obtain a notebook, lined or unlined, to be your journal. How will you log your journey? Record your personal observations.

- Relax. Forget about spelling, grammar, or neatness. This is for you alone.
- You do not need to make corrections. A so-called "error" might reveal something important.
- You can begin by describing where you are, or even "I am writing and I don't have a clue..."
- Use your normal language.
- Sketch, draw maps, paste pictures in your journal.

Creating a log of your journey will help you chart your personal inner landscape.

Physical Awareness

Physical awareness is fundamental to knowing where you stand. Start by exploring the terrain of the sensual body. Cultivate an awareness of touch, taste, sight, smell, and hearing. What draws you? What disturbs you? Some of us who have been estranged from authentic desire for too long may have become desensitized to our authentic selves.

Explore physical awareness with breath, movement, walking, and dance. Make an inventory of personal pleasures. Consider these ways to reconnect to your own true self.

- Experience your body through bathing, swimming and hot springs.

- Notice what sights inspire you, calm you, or bring up any feelings.
- Walk barefoot and dig in your garden.
- Exert yourself in movement. Sweat.
- Enjoy sensual touch, self-pleasure, or pleasuring another.
- Stretch, do yoga, feel texture against skin.
- Enjoy the scent of the sea, plant fragrances, and the tang of wood smoke.
- Listen to birdsong, the ocean, wind in the trees, music that moves you, and your own voice singing.
- Enjoy flavors and textures through mindful tasting.

What enlivens your sensual body?

Other ways to explore physical awareness are the body scan meditation and progressive relaxation. The body scan meditation gently guides us in mindful awareness and inquiry and is taught by meditation practitioners and health care professionals. Jon Kabat-Zinn explains this practice at length in his wise and practical book *Full Catastrophe Living*.

Progressive relaxation is a guided exercise of tensing and relaxing muscles in a gentle and deliberate way, and is taught by Dr. Herbert Benson and Miriam Z. Klipper in their groundbreaking book *The Relaxation Response*.

As well as enhancing self-awareness, both practices also offer health benefits such as lower blood pressure and less chronic pain, by reducing tension and stress. Community health education programs often teach these practices as part of a wellness curriculum.

Cultivate Emotional Awareness

We are beings who feel deeply, no matter that some of us think we need to "keep calm and carry on." Culture dictates what we should consider an appropriate expressive style for a man or a woman. Authentic feelings may be hidden behind masks of social convention. To examine what lies hidden behind such masks, we can begin to explore our inner emotional landscape with gentleness and compassion. One way to develop a gentle way of being is to see yourself as a young child and imagine how you would want to be cared for. Find a photograph of yourself as a child. Extend loving kindness to this tender soul. You might also hold a symbol of yourself by using a cuddly toy like a baby bear, cat, dolphin, or whatever might symbolize your younger inner self.

Develop compassion by consciously practicing loving-kindness with yourself and with others. A Buddhist meditation gives the example of radiating kindness with a boundless heart, as a mother with her only child. Find a comfortable quiet place and allow your body to relax. Let loving-kindness fill your heart.

May I be safe from inner and outer harm.
May I be happy and peaceful.
May I be healthy and strong.
May I be able to take care of myself, joyfully.

With a gentle breath and soft heart recite these phrases for developing loving-kindness. The words can be adapted to feel easy and right for you. Try practicing this for ten or fifteen minutes and let the words sink in. This practice can also be extended toward those you love as well as those you find difficult by saying to yourself, "May (the person) be safe from inner and outer harm." In *The Art of Forgiveness, Lovingkindness, and Peace*, psychologist Jack

Kornfield provides stories and practices to cultivate peace and support healing.

Being able to connect with and express our authentic feelings can enrich our relationships and create depth in our life. Explore your emotional landscape.

- In a journal, record your how you feel.
- Practice loving-kindness.
- Write a letter to a person who has hurt you, and then burn the letter.
- Explore unspoken feelings with finger paints and clay.
- Embody feelings with movement.
- Go jogging to discharge adrenaline, or pound a pillow or the floor to release intense emotions.
- Cry freely in a safe place.
- Laugh until you cry.
- Talk. Talk to your dog, your cat, the trees, the stones, the storm. Talk to your loved ones.

Counselors and psychotherapists can help by offering many ways to support self-expression and dialogue.

Mental Awareness

Thoughts shape beliefs and actions. Your self-concept is a collection of beliefs built from experience and social learning. It answers the question "Who am I?" and includes past, present, and future selves. We constantly assess ourselves. What we think about ourselves influences our behaviors and emotions.

Self-concept includes internalized messages or identities adopted from others. An example of this are the gender roles and expectations we learn as young children. Learned roles can be comfortable, or they may not be a good fit. Sometimes a person can become aware of a thought pattern that does not feel right. How do your thoughts shape your actions and life direction? What influence do these ideas have on how you see yourself?

Negative thoughts can arise from an internal critic. Journaling a dialogue with the critic can help identify the voice. Ask yourself when you first heard these words, what was the purpose? Do you need these words now? Who is the critic? What is different about you and your situation now? It may be that strong cautions you heard in childhood no longer serve you as an adult, or words that wounded long ago no longer hold power.

By examining your thoughts in a journal, you can reflect on what has brought you to the present point. Writing a personal narrative, the story of your life, allows you to reflect on experiences and influences as well as the roads taken and not taken. Because your journal is private, you can examine your life with complete honesty. Begin at the beginning, and write freely without editing. Attend with compassion. Stay curious. Note what themes are constant. Note your values, your challenges, and reactions. Your story matters because you matter.

Reflect on your present and past self, and explore what you want in the future. What would be an ideal day from beginning to end? What would you consider to be your right livelihood, right relationship, and good health? Athletes use visualization to shape future performances and imagine a successful outcome. Visualize your ideal self.

The unconscious is also a powerful source of information. Explore your dreams and discover what lies deep within. Keep a journal at your bedside and, after waking from a dream, record as many details as you can. The story your dream tells may provide insight, inspiration, or information about where you are in life now. Consider the meaning of your dreams. Deepen your understanding by looking into the well of your unconscious. Robert A. Johnson, Jungian psychotherapist, discusses the dream journal and dream interpretation in his book, *Inner Work: Using Dreams and Active Imagination for Personal Growth.*

Practice Spiritual Awareness

"Spirit" has been deemed so essential to life that people around the world use a word for it that also means "breath." The Latin "spiritus," Hebrew "ruah," and Arabic "ruh" all mean "breath." In Chinese it is "ch'i" that means "life force, breath." We are only alive with the "breath" of "spirit."

Finding one's spiritual true north is a lifelong process and can lead down countless paths. One can follow or renew spiritual practices of the family culture. One can choose an established religion and participate in the spiritual community. Or one can follow a highly personalized spiritual journey and adopt practices from different traditions. Still, some people do not consider themselves spiritual, but are enlightened by modern science and might think of creation as a humming web of energy linking all things, as described by physicist Fritjof Capra in the *Tao of Physics*.

Many spiritual teachers have sought guidance through solitude in nature. Moses sought God alone on Mount Sinai. Jesus went into the emptiness of the desert. Buddha sat solitary in the forest to seek enlightenment. Muhammad went alone into the mountain cave at Jabal an-Nour.

"Ask, and it shall be given you; seek, and ye shall find; knock, and it shall be opened unto you," says the Bible. There are many ways to seek guidance.

- Ask, pray, and talk with spirit.
- Chant, sing, dance.
- Create an altar or ritual tools.
- Invoke, celebrate, do ceremony, give thanks.
- Write it out. Paint or draw.

How do you speak with spirit?

I remember hiking Mt. Takao, a sacred mountain near Tokyo, Japan. It was dusk, and in the darkening shadows I came to a waterfall marked sacred by Shinto rice-straw ropes. Shinto is the indigenous nature-based religion of Japan. On a flat granite rock facing the waterfall, an old woman in a kimono lit a long, folded white paper. Fire burned down to her fingertips and she tossed the ashes into the air. I can only imagine she was sending up a written prayer to the gods.

Meditation

Meditation, also known as contemplation, is an ancient spiritual practice found in many cultures. Essentially, it involves clearing the mind and inducing a certain mode of consciousness in an effort to develop such traits as reverence and awareness, or attitudes such as compassion, forgiveness, and inner peace. "Meditation" comes from a Latin word meaning "to think, contemplate, devise, ponder." Meditation can include repetitive sacred words, prayers, and movement, and certain practices require years of dedication. The well-known psychologist Lawrence LeShan provides an excellent introduction to this art in his book, *How to Meditate.*

A meditation on the breath is a simple way to begin to calm the "monkey mind."

Sit comfortably.
Your back is straight, hands and arms relaxed,
jaws and shoulders relaxed.
Your eyes are half closed, with diffuse focus.
Take a slow, deep breath in for a count of four,
hold for a count of one,
breathe out slowly for a count of four.
Feel your shoulders drop.
Soften your belly and breathe naturally.
Notice your inhale and exhale.
Breathe normally and notice your breath.
When your mind wanders,
return your attention to your breath.
Just easy.
Repeat a focusing word, mantra, or prayer if you wish.
Do this for as long or as little as you like.
You are gently aware.

Finding true north is essential for accurate navigation. Your journey begins from your own true north. Find it.

Pause for a moment and reflect:

- Do you have a journal?

- How do you record your thoughts and feelings? Do you always write, have you considered other ways?

- How do you feel in your body? How do you honor and care for your physical self?

- What emotions long to be expressed? What will allow for this expression?

- How do you explore your mental self?

- What place does the spiritual have in your life? How do you express this?

The Land

CHAPTER 3

The Land

THE LAND CALLS TO you. Go out on the land to listen and learn. The land calls in the voice of liquid water and frog song, in birdsong and the whisper of wind through fir, spruce, pine, and oak. Hawk dips a wing in blessing, and the open sky can make the way clear or wrap you in a blanket of mist.

Be still and listen. Slow down, sit, clear your mind. Listen. Stillness allows you to see more. Learn what nature has to teach. Cycles of abundance and scarcity, cycles of migration, cycles of mating, of birthing, of building, of resting. What cycle of life are you in, how does your life flow? Birth, death, and renewal; what are the lessons of the cycles? Learn intimately from one place, one personal place of power. Learn what nature has to teach you about yourself.

One Wild Place

A naturalist has the practice of regularly visiting one wild place over time to study the habitat. Naturalists call it a sit spot. Find a place close enough to your home that you can visit on a regular basis and come to know intimately. Visit as often as you can – weekly or even a few times a month would be wonderful. Go at different times of the day, early and late, to see what is different. Record what you see, make note of the plants and animals. Deepen your understanding of nature.

Many urban areas support regional parks. Go to a nearby park or beach, someplace you can get to easily, with as much solitude as you can find. Even a spot in the backyard will do, especially if you have some wilder parts. I use the wildland outside my backyard fence. I can drag a chair out there and visit the oak woodland. Growing up in the city, I took a bus or walked the five miles to the regional park. If your spot is in a public park, you can maintain a mindset of focus that indicates to passersby that you are occupied. Sometimes carrying a notebook will suggest you are about a task and would like to be left alone. Notice what direction you are called to face. What meaning does that hold for you? Are you are called to a high place? Or a low place? What does your chosen environment reveal about you?

Safety

Choose a place where you will feel comfortable being alone. If you do not feel comfortable alone, find a partner to accompany you. You can find a sit spot at some distance from your partner that feels safe to you, but will still allow for quiet and the ability to experience nature intimately. Go at your own pace.

Tell a friend or family member where you will be, when you will return, and generally what you will do. Plan to check in with them when you return. They can call for help if they do not hear from you. To be receptive to subtle thoughts and impressions, and to be safe in your surroundings, plan to be clean and sober. Leave any electronics in the car, or at least turned off (unless there's an emergency). Consider the role of your "check-in" buddy. Do they hold you in heart and mind in other ways? Who do you hold in your heart?

Physical Preparation for the Outdoors

Choose a terrain that is approachable, an area in which you are comfortable. For unknown territories, take a map and review any available park descriptions.

Get a general idea of the habitat. Will you be on a beach with changing tides? In chaparral with ticks? In a desert area with cactus? If you are in landslide country, be cautious after a rain, when there might be falling rocks, mudslides, or falling trees. Get to know poisonous plants such as poison oak and ivy. Study a local trail guide or a naturalist's field guide.

Familiarize yourself with your wild neighbors and get some idea of how best to handle a potential encounter. Ask park personnel for advice. Know the poisonous snakes in your area. Rattlesnakes are out and about in different seasons, and the watchword is to look where you walk and sit. Learning the habits of wild neighbors will help you recognize their presence even if you cannot always see them. If you become familiar with nests, burrows, and markings, you can have some idea of who is present.

Usually, a large mammal sighting will be a rare, miraculous encounter. But know how to be safe just in case. Do not run from mountain lions: you know how cats love to chase. Make yourself look bigger than an easy meal. In bear country use your jacket and raise your arms to make yourself look as large as you can. Stag and ram in rut may be more aggressive. Parks often post instructions on how to handle wildlife encounters safely. I find that keeping calm and allowing the animal to go about their business allows us to be mutually respectful. Discover your own best response. When such a meeting happens, ask what importance that animal holds for you. Do you have a special affinity?

Weather changes all the time. I tend to think of weather forecasters as seers who cast bones to predict the future. While you will know what to wear for the season, be prepared for the weather to change and for unexpected events. Wear comfortable shoes, bring water and a snack. A watch will allow you to time your walk so you can return before dark, if that is your plan. Always carry a day pack with a jacket, hat, knife, and water, and if you're going to be out late in the day a flashlight is a good idea. If you are prepared for the weather, a day spent in the rain can be magical.

There's always a chance that you might injure yourself and have to return at a slower pace, or you could encounter another sort of delay, so you should be prepared to spend some time outdoors after sundown. If you've told a friend about your plans, and you have missed an agreed-on check-in, your friend will know that you have not returned and can get help. How much gear do you take? Is it enough? Is it too much? How comfortable are you in your own skin? How capable do you feel? Go slowly and progress at your own pace.

Respect the Environment

Respect Mother Nature and you will be respected in return. You may even witness an arc of the "circle of life" when one life is taken to sustain another. Remember, that is the grand design and holds a lesson. There is a greater wisdom at work here, respect the events that unfold. Give thanks. What feeds you? Who do you feed?

How do you support the earth and her people? Be attentive to the wild community and its needs. You might want to take home a shed antler or some other interesting natural object, but consider how nature cycles everything through with purpose. What plants or animals rely on the minerals provided by that antler? Reflect on how your presence might affect a feeding or nesting time or if harvesting a wild plant might reduce an important food resource.

Respecting the environment means leaving the place as it is, or better. Leave no trace. The Leave No Trace outdoor and wilderness ethics guidelines call for minimum human impact on nature. If your stay is overlong and you cannot get to a port-a-potty or toilet, you may need to find another way to eliminate. Leaving no trace calls for packing out any debris, so take a small plastic bag for this purpose and dispose of your waste in the trash when you leave.

Noticing

Notice your surroundings, the slow track of shadow and light, the terrain, the vegetation. Learn to recognize the rustle of birds in the brush, the breathing of pine trees, and the birdsong. Use your whole body to feel the wind, the sun and shade on your skin. Feel the texture of the bark. What tree is dormant and what tree is dying? Feel the earth with your bare feet and bare hands.

Move slowly. Watch how deer move, how long they stand and graze, and when they lie down. For the most part, animals tend to move slowly, are often still, and carefully notice everything. If you move quickly you will be less likely to see the wildlife around you. Be aware of your own breath, your own heartbeat. The tracker is an observer of everything.

In his *Field Guide to Nature Observation and Tracking,* Tom Brown, Jr. writes that tracking is not just about seeing footprints in the dirt, but is also about reading the stories told by the wind and water, grass, trees, and soil. Everything that moves tells a story. Every track is linked to every other track. The tracker's footprint is woven into the print of the one that is being tracked. Brown writes that, "No story in nature exists independently. Everything is related."

You will soon recognize the ones who come calling. Walk around and get to know your neighborhood. Then sit still. See what action starts up once you stop. Intense watchfulness will get the bobcat her dinner. Know for certain that you are being watched as well. As a frequent visitor to my sit spot, I got to know a young coyote. He would trail me for a ways and when I stopped to look back, he'd sit, yawn, and look away. We kept up this walking companionship for a while. Wild friendships are beautiful, but for their sake, keep them wild.

Breathe in, inhale black sage and mugwort, breathe out, you are also inhaled. Breathe in, breathe out. Reflect inward, reflect outward. Attend to your surroundings, safety, and your physical body. Attend to inspiration and impressions. Keep a record of your thoughts and experiences, and sketches of what you see and find. Recording your observations will help you to see deeply and notice things that you might otherwise overlook. The practice will hone your ability to look outside yourself and reflect on life. Develop an intimate relationship with the land, and become aware of self and what the natural world has to tell you. Plants and animals, soil and sky tell a story about place, cycles of change and interwoven relationships. No longer strangers, you begin to learn the language of the borderlands, that edge between worlds and the place of transformation.

Pause for a moment and reflect:

- Is there one wild place that calls to you?

- Who will be your check-in buddy when you are on the land?

- What does your chosen environment reveal about you?

- What do you have in your day pack?

- Can you draw a map of your sit spot?

The Four Directions

CHAPTER 4

The Four Directions

OUR ANCESTORS STUDIED THE world and noticed the patterns of things. They witnessed the cycling of seasons, the wheel of turning stars, the circle of horizons, and observed the four directions. Practically every culture on earth has identified the cardinal directions. Ancient people marked the points of the rising and setting suns. They noticed that with a quarter turn you find the North Star. From this, the fourth direction can be inferred. Migrating and hunting people have survived this way for thousands of years.

Directional guides vary across cultures. The Chinese four directions are guarded by the Azure Dragon of the East, the Vermilion Bird of the South, the White Tiger of the West, and the Black Turtle of the North. The directions also correspond with the four seasons, and the elements of wood, fire, metal, and water, placing the earth at the center. Some cultures use the directions not only to find their place on the land but also to find their way through life. The mandala of India represents the cosmos and the wheel of life. It includes reference points for the four directions and for different aspects of the human being.

The four directions have been meaningful as an instructional tool for personal and spiritual development. Use of the four directions model can be directly experienced, and is suited to self-exploration under the open sky. In *The Red Road to Wellbriety*, published by the White Bison organization for Native American recovery, the Medicine Wheel teachings of the four directions are offered as a guide to healing and recovery. Using the cyclical model found in nature, White Bison suggests some attributes of the four directions:

> East – Spring season, emotional growth, individual healing
> South – Summer season, mental growth, family healing
> West – Fall season, physical growth, community healing
> North – Winter season, spiritual growth, Nation healing

For readers who are unfamiliar with Four Directions or Medicine Wheel teachings, Steven Foster and Meredith Little, founders of the School of Lost Borders, describe a similar way to understand human nature and development in their book, *The Four Shields: The Initiatory Seasons of Human Nature*. Taking the suggestions of Foster and Little we can consider how the four directions might be used as a guide.

The East

The East is where the sun rises. It is renewal after the long dark. The rising sun is a powerful symbol of opening and creation. It is visionary and far seeing. It is freshness and new life. Spring lives in the East.

The South

Heat comes from the South. It can represent the raw energies of feeling and the physical body. Summer lives in the South.

The West

The West is where the sun goes down and darkness enters. It is an inward-turning place of dreams and reflection, depth and introspection. Fall lives in the West.

The North

The North requires action for us to survive the cold. Such action requires responsibility and understanding. It knows how to manifest and make things happen. Winter lives in the North.

NORTH
Winter

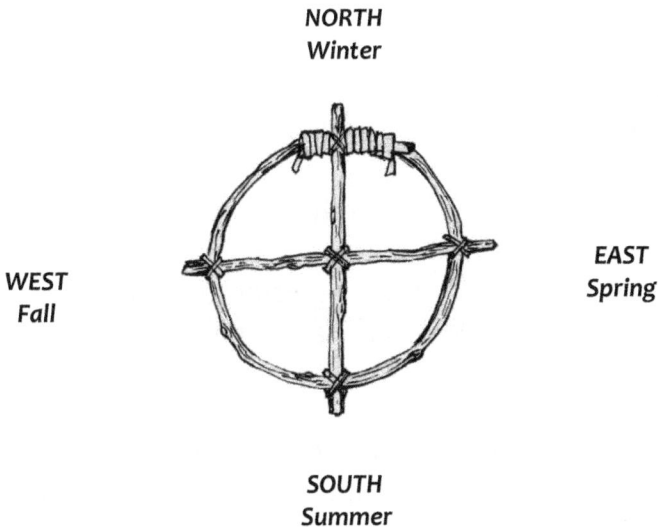

EAST
Spring

WEST
Fall

SOUTH
Summer

If we look at the general characteristics of the directions, or shields, it is possible to find parallel attributes in ourselves or in our current way of being. For example, a person who has strong characteristics of an Eastern Shield might be highly involved in spiritual practices. If someone is over-identified with the Eastern Shield they may be described as "airy" or not very realistic.

The Four Shields approach is a simple and valuable tool for self-exploration and development. To work with the Four Shields, explore the characteristics that best describe you, explore what Shield most closely describes your personality. There are many ways to learn from this. For example, using the Four Shields for growth and self-development can create more balance. A person who identifies strongly with the South may feel that exaggerated spontaneity has led to chaos in their relationships and work. This person may choose to create more balance in their Western aspect by practicing more thoughtful pursuits. Taking time to journal and think through the choices and actions will bring greater balance to the West. Therapy or any practice for self-reflection would also strengthen the Western aspects.

The teachings of the four directions can be used as a process to help solve a problem. Consider a matter you are struggling with. Begin with the South.

1. South: Begin by considering the Southern aspects. How do you feel about the matter emotionally, how do you feel in your body?

2. West: Consider the Western aspects. Sit with your true feelings and think through the matter at hand. What meaning or lesson might the matter hold? What might be the origins, what are possible ways to resolve the matter? Perhaps sleep on it.

3. North: Consider the Northern aspects. With your knowledge and understanding, what will you do? Take action.

4. East: Consider what spiritual or ritual act will best mark this journey. Give thanks, enact the ceremony and honor spirit.

Erin, who tried this process of working with the four directions, said, "Many things in my life get started and never end, but this has a beginning and an end. This allows for completion, and I can do this myself. There is no giving away power." The circular nature of this process also encourages you to continue in your understanding.

Go out on the land. Are you called to a certain direction? Do you hold a question that pertains to a certain direction? Set out in that direction, holding that question or need. Does one aspect of your self need more healing and balance? Start there and move sun-wise or clockwise around the wheel to the next direction.

We'll look at this with Jack, who shared this story with me.

Jack's Story

Jack was a husband, father, and dedicated breadwinner for his family of four. Although his wife also worked, he always felt he was "bottom-line responsible" for his family's welfare. In his own childhood his mother worked to pay the bills while his father was a perpetual graduate student. In contrast to his father, Jack felt it important that he take full responsibility for supporting his family, even if it meant sacrificing his personal needs and his health. He described himself as quiet and hardworking, and he felt marginalized in a difficult work situation.

Jack wanted to develop more balance and get unstuck from a hyper-responsible Northern shield. He worked in the Eastern aspects of ceremony and spirit by creating a ritual to challenge expectations of himself. Jack planned to spend a day in solitude in a remote national park.

I went to the Bristlecone Pine Forest, the Methuselah Grove. The park sign said the bristlecone pines are four to five thousand years old. The trail was uphill and steep. I watched the sun rise and felt I needed to sing that Cherokee Dawn song. I was unsure about being so loud in the quiet morning but then I realized this was a rule to break about my own silence.

I came to a bristlecone on a ledge facing east with a sharp drop down to the desert floor. I talked to Bristlecone. She said get naked and expose yourself. I laughed. She said I am here exposed and beautiful and ancient. It was true, there was this beautiful, ancient tree, standing alone on the ledge. It had stood up to thousands of years of exposure to wind and snow. I thanked Bristlecone and poured water.

Jack heard the lesson of being seen and heard as his true self. When he came back to the group, this quiet, thoughtful man offered a song in his ancestral language of the Abenaki of New England. Afterward, he said he felt more able to speak with his own voice.

Above and Below

A world without shadow is flat. In the light, we see a pretty fair representation of the world we live in, and so it is with ourselves. For the most part, we are known by how we present ourselves. However, just as plants are sustained by an underground root system, below ground, in the dark, the seeds of soul germinate.

Carl Jung, psychiatrist and founder of analytic psychotherapy, used the term "shadow" to represent the parts of ourselves that we keep hidden. These may be parts of ourselves that we consider less than noble or that have been suppressed by the culture in which we live. Simple awareness and recognition of these shadows can bring about understanding.

Often we can identify our personal shadow by thinking about a time when somebody set off a strong negative feeling that we felt was alien. One way to explore your shadow self is to consider a trait that you disdain in others. Think of your hot buttons and emotional triggers. Use art and writing to explore this trait and thoughtfully consider the presence of this quality in yourself. You may extend a loving-kindness meditation toward that part of yourself and the meaning it holds for you. Acknowledging a discounted anger may reveal an unknown strength or, conversely, lowering the shield of anger may allow a tender heart to come forward. Being able to see into your own darkness with courage and compassion allows you to see others with equal consideration. To explore this in greater depth, read *Meeting the Shadow: The Hidden Power of the Dark Side of Human Nature*, edited by Connie Zweig and Jeremiah Abrams.

Using the Four Shields as a guide, see what characteristics are most strongly represented in yourself. Which aspects are least developed? In what way can you create a more balanced shield? Go out on the land to explore.

Pause for a moment and reflect:

- How do you orient yourself to the Four Directions on the land?

- Consider your personal characteristics, are there certain attributes that stand out?

- In what area would you like to have more balance?

- Use the wheel of the Four Directions to explore your characteristics.

- Consider your shadow self, how would you begin a dialogue?

- How would you hold yourself with compassion?

Maps for Spirit

CHAPTER 5

Maps for Spirit

WE ARE ON THE trail. Right habitat, nose to ground. In the brush, the undergrowth is dense. No footprint yet but we are in the right place during the right season. If we are patient, we will catch a glimpse of the quarry. However, we need not rely on luck; our efforts can be rewarded with greater ease and surety than just being in the right place at the right time. There are maps for tracking soul.

Ceremony and ritual help with attunement and map out a path to follow. In the practice of tracking soul, our senses are sharper when we are quiet and attuned. We are able to hear the voice on the wind, and to see the faint message left in the sand. Ritual and ceremony bring focus to the work. Confirmations, Holy Communion, New Year rituals of renewal, or silent retreat can help access spirit. Small, personal rituals bring a sense of order to our days. A daily evening stroll or Sunday sit-down dinner with the family are personal rituals. We have private spiritual rituals of prayer and meditation. We already know how to create personal rituals that bring meaning and depth to life.

An intentional ritual, like a pilgrimage, has a beginning, middle, and end. Or, sometimes, as the oldest stories tell us, the journey begins at the end. Ancient tales teach the cycle of life and death and life. We see this all around in the natural world and it is reflected in the world's oldest beliefs about transformation through life, death, and rebirth. It is our most cherished story and it brings a message of hope in our darkest hours.

Classic models of transformation and rites of passage can be found throughout the world. Ethnographer Arnold van Gennep wrote about this more than a hundred years ago in his book, *The Rites of Passage.* Transitions and transformations begin with an ending or separation. The bones of ceremony are found in the old stories. The hero leaves the known world, Odysseus leaves Thrace, Alice tumbles down the rabbit hole. Sometimes we are snatched up and dropped down on a dark path not of our own making. The world is turned upside down and we are by the side of an unknown road with a thorny thicket behind us and a dark wood ahead.

In the transformational journey we leave the ordinary world, which has been our habitat and habit of being, and make a clear crossing into a different space. We cross the threshold and enter a place separate from the old activities of life. This is where the real business of change takes place. Strange creatures appear in this new landscape, we take on new tasks, and we are tested. In some ways we become a spirit being. Again, the old stories show us this pattern of withdrawal and return, as in Christ in the Desert or Buddha in the Forest.

Finally, we Return. We come home renewed and with a truer vision for ourselves. We return with a message or new understanding to incorporate into the world. We bring back a gift for our people.

Earth Walk

The earth walk is a dawn-to-dusk ritual journey taken under the open sky that mirrors the journey of exploration to meet soul. Like many rituals, it is an act taken in time and space that reflects an inner journey of spirit. One such example is the coming-of-age Australian walkabout in which an adolescent makes a physical journey in the outback that is an enactment of his spiritual and social journey to manhood. The earth walk journey is taught by the School of Lost Borders, at Big Pine, California, as the Medicine Walk.

The Aboriginal walkabout, the First Nations or Native American vision quest, and other traditional rites of passage ceremonies usually require months or even years of preparation and are performed within a traditional community. The day-long practice of solitude in the wild offered by the earth walk allows us the time and space to explore self and soul in the mirror of nature and renew our deepest connections.

The pattern of the earth walk journey can easily follow the basic pattern of a rite of passage, which provides for a severance or departure from the ordinary, crossing the threshold into a sacred space, and return. Consider how you might use ritual to mark each transition of your journey.

Severance

To begin with, rituals of severance mark what we are letting go, and what we will leave behind. Such rituals can include getting rid of things, cleaning, cleansing, cutting off, burning, casting off, fasting, or abstaining from certain foods or drinks. Clearing away and cleaning are concrete tasks that make space for receiving, in both the mind and spirit.

Threshold

Now, having made ourselves free to depart, we can cross the threshold. We cross clearly and consciously into the borderlands. Crossing the threshold in the earth walk, we draw a line in the dirt or lay a stick down and step over; or enter a circle of stones and cross over. Crossing the threshold can be as simple as a bow to indicate that you are ready to begin the journey into the borderlands.

Return

Having spent time in the borderlands, consulting with its inhabitants and completing the tasks, we return. When returning, bring back a representation of your time in the threshold, a talisman or reminder. Bring back a name, a story, a song.

Incorporation

Now comes the real work. We return home to family and bring our vision into the world. Bring your gift back to your people. Build an altar, create a touchstone or symbol of your gift. Your task is to live out the vision.

Use personal ritual to clarify and signal the task you are to undertake. Use any ritual that calls you. Each culture has an indigenous tradition that was learned and expressed by community elders. We are all indigenous to this Earth. Your ancestors invite you to learn their ancient ways.

A Note about Culture

Linda's Story

A Japanese-American woman was drawn to nature and inspired by books and stories about Native American culture. She learned shamanic drumming and describes her experience in a trance-like drum journey this way.

> I traveled to the underworld and found myself dodging tectonic plates and magma until I reached the surface of the other side of the planet. I was in a misty forest of cedar with little undergrowth. A mature wood, with trees widely spaced. I stood at the bottom of a hill and saw narrow stone stairs leading up the hill into the mist. Climbing the stairs, I saw a tall torii gate, or Japanese portal to a Shinto shrine. On the other side of the gate was an ancient Japanese shamaness wearing a bear skin.

Linda had found her way to the indigenous shamanic practices of her own people who have their own powerful relationship with the spirits of nature.

When you claim your culture, you have access to your personal indigenous heritage. Often it takes very little digging to learn about your own rich traditions. Yoruba practitioners can be found in Manhattan and Oakland, Celtic traditions are celebrated around the United States, and Conchero Aztec communities are found throughout the West. Powwows, tribal organizations, and Indian Health

Service clinics offer ways to reconnect with traditional practices.

If possible, talk with the elders of your family or your cultural center. In recent history, indigenous earth-based practices were crushed by armies and other forms of oppression, so some traditions have gone into hiding. As a student, be respectful and patient when asking for information. Elders may be reluctant to share information that tradition-keepers maintain as sacred or requiring protection. Sometimes you can apprentice to a traditional art, such as martial arts, powwow sings, or wildcrafting, and become known as dedicated and trusted to receive the sacred stories. I once attended a storytelling event where one of the storytellers invited me to learn a song of my people. Our languages are precious, and some of them are now rarely heard. Learn a song of your people in the original language. Keep the songs alive.

Ritual Tasks

Ritual tasks make visible our intention. Symbolic acts give meaning and strengthen emotional involvement. An example of this is the lighting of a candle at an altar to accompany prayer. We have celebratory rituals and rituals for luck. We have rituals of grief. In some ways, we are all wounded. Cultures suffer ongoing wounds from oppression. Enslavement and genocide tear apart and destroy families, languages, and cultural practices. Grief and wounding that is unspoken can lead to depression, disease, suicide, mental illness, drug abuse, and addiction. People can try to dull the pain or escape it entirely. Wounds from relationships turn into rancor, bitterness, anger, sarcasm, and more broken relationships. Wounds can also tell us that old ways are ready to die.

Story teller and psychoanalyst Clarissa Pinkola Estés explains the healing power of attending to grief. In her book, *Women Who Run with the Wolves*, she offers the practice of the descansos. The descansos are the highway crosses and flowers throughout the Southwest that mark where people have died on a road. They originally indicated the "resting places" between church and cemetery. To use the model of descansos as a personal practice, tell the story of your wounding and mark the "little deaths" in your life. Healing comes with open-eyed examination, telling the story, and of finally grieving what has too often been pushed away, buried lonely and voiceless.

During your earth walk, go out and speak with a wounded part of yourself.

The Heart Broken Open

This is the task: go into nature to attend to your wounding. Find a wound in the earth. It can be any broken-open place, exposed roots of a fallen tree, a lightning strike, ravine, or rent in the earth. Speak your own hurt into the earth. Begin the dialogue with your wound. Feel your feelings. Know that your story is being heard. Talk to spirit. Ask for help. Give thanks. Listen and observe. Pay attention to any impression or image that is offered to you.

Ask, what is the gift in the wound? What is transformative? Or, just be heard.

Pause for a moment and reflect:

- What personal rituals do you have now?

- Is there some transformation or life stage you would like to mark? What rituals would be most appropriate?

- What is your cultural lineage? Are there special aspects of your heritage that speak to you? How could you learn more?

- What in your life has broken open your heart, your soul? How will you bear witness? Who, human or more-than-human, will offer loving witness to your story?

The Borderlands

CHAPTER 6

The Borderlands

IN TRACKING SOUL, WE track the edge of worlds. We are in the borderlands, standing between one world and the next, in a place of transition and transformation. We are no longer, but also not yet. Senses sharpen, the hair stands up on the back of our necks. The world is bright with magic and all of nature speaks to us. The earth walk takes place in the borderlands. This is where adventure begins.

You find yourself in strange territory; how do you find your bearings? Who left these markings? How do you read the signs? If we practice looking for faint signs and learn their meaning, then what starts as a thin, faint track becomes thicker and clearer as we go along. Myths and stories tell us what to look for. Stories from many cultures provide a map to this lost art, tell us that we once understood the speech of animals and spirits. The key to the language of the borderlands lies in intuition, wide perception, deep listening, imagination, myth and dream.

Entering the borderlands, what do we do? Just as in any new territory: stop, sense, notice, and be aware. Use the skills of observation you know from being in your sit spot.

Use all your senses and be grounded in the present, in the moment, here and now.

Practice the skills of being grounded. Have someone read the instructions aloud, record them for yourself, or read them yourself so you can recall them.

Grounding

Whether standing, sitting, or lying down, be comfortable, relaxed, and in contact with the earth.

Stretch your arms and legs, roll your head.

With a soft belly, breathe slowly and notice your inhale and exhale.

Take a deep breath, exhale and feel your shoulders drop.

Breathe in slowly through your nose for a count of four.

Pause for a count of one.

Exhale slowly for a count of four.

Relax your jaw.

Repeat and notice how your body feels.

Notice the details of what is around you.

Touch the cool earth, the sand, the chair's surface.

Notice the feel of sun or shade on your body.

Use all your senses: touch, sound, smell, taste, and sight.

Thump your heels on the ground and feel them.

Say to yourself, "I am grounded."

Visualize your spine as a strong tree trunk;

your roots going down deep into the earth,

a strong, solid base;

your branches extending upwards through your body.

Your breathing is soft and relaxed.

Notice how you feel.

Feel the weight of your body, feel your back against the chair or tree.

You are connected to the world.

In the borderlands, soul is waiting to speak with you, show you, be with you. Your soul's story may be expressed visually, or through impressions, language, channeled writing, dreams, painting, music, or any number of other ways. Ask your questions. Listen for answers. The answer and language is specific to you. See the gifts.

To be receptive to the language of the borderlands, you can practice seeing with different eyes, hearing your inner voice, and understanding the language of story through creative visualization. Practice at home in a quiet, safe, undisturbed place. Your personal experience may be visual, auditory, kinesthetic, or come through another sense that is strong in you.

Visualization

Relax. Lie on your back in a comfortable position. Use pillows to create comfort, place a scarf over your eyes, stretch and relax your muscles, and take a few slow, deep breaths. In your mind's eye visualize a place in nature near a pond or lake. It can be a place you know or have seen in a picture. The place is peaceful, restful, and safe. You feel at home and comfortable here. There are no buildings around, only a small rowboat or canoe waiting for you on the quiet shore. Take time to appreciate your waterside surroundings. What is the weather like? How is the temperature? What plants do you see? What is underfoot? What do you smell? What do you hear? Do you feel movement of air over your skin? Take your time and fill in all the details you can. Go to the boat and climb in. Sit and relax. Hear the lapping of the water against the hull. Magically, the boat drifts toward the opposite shore. You enjoy the movement across the shallow water, the touch of wind, the freshness of the air. You are relaxed and interested in all that is around you. You reach the shore and the boat slides onto the slope of a sandy beach. You get out and look around. Again, notice what is around you. A figure approaches. You wonder if this is the teacher or guide you have been looking for. The figure gets close enough for you to make out its appearance. The figure stands in front of you. You ask, "Are you my teacher?" Wait for the answer. Listen to the response. If the answer is no, continue to wait and ask until you meet your teacher. Then ask your teacher, "What are you here to tell me?" Listen carefully. Give your thanks. Return to the boat, which will magically take you back across the water to the shore where you step out. Thank the boat and everything around you. When you are ready to return to the room, open your eyes. Write down your experience.

Your teacher may not appear as you would imagine. You can ask, why you? The particular presentation will hold some meaning for you. Just as I experienced in Yosemite's back country, I had spent so much time in the company of bears that when I encountered a cougar in the dead of night I assumed that the shadow that leapt off a boulder to land so silently was a bear. Although my experience with Cougar was in real time, I will never forget the lesson that I could not see Cougar because I was expecting Bear. Expect the unexpected.

Take your practice outside. Enter with respect, give thanks, and give your greeting. Ask your questions. Listen for answers. Censor nothing. Animals speak. The Spring is Holy. The Sea is your Mother. Stone is your Ancestor. Bones speak your story. Story creates meaning and the pattern of your life reveals itself.

Monique tells what she experienced in the borderlands.

Turning toward the eastern trail to begin an upward climb, I see the disjointed remains of a deer. Continuing along the river toward an ocean view, a flattened glade and more remains of a deadly struggle, feathers and down litter the flattened grass. There are no other body parts except for one exquisite fully fanned-out wing of an owl -- a disturbingly happy find. Even to my uneducated eye this is a sacred object, a gift.

The wandering along the beach. I was intent on discovering a talisman to bring home to share. The beach provided me dried kelp globes I fitted with driftwood handles and filled with pebbles to make rattles.

Climbing east through the oak trees the final three hours. I picked up acorns. Renewal. More gifts with purpose.

The last four years in my own life have had their share of distress and dismemberment. My own failed marriage, my closest friend's lost job, home, and focus. The take away: a solo run through wood, river, and ocean that mirrored my personal effort to make lives whole again. The day and guidance made it clear that there was distress, but it was also clear there were gifts of the sacred and renewal. Thank you!

The act of creation is another way to call in soul. Choose to work with the dawn or the dusk, with the edges of horizons, at the shore or on the mountain top. Create in the margins to learn about the borderlands. This is a good way to stay conscious of the fact that you are in the between, at the edge of worlds. Be conscious of being in that space.

Create a talisman, prayer flag, or prayer stick of your story. The winding round and round of string and the repeated threading of beads can be a meditation. Every turn of your wrist is a prayer, every wind of yarn around your prayer stick a petition, every twist of sweet grass a whisper of gratitude.

Be open to meaning. Practice to gain skill. Review your day and encounters. What did Crow say as you were heading out? From whom was the gift of the falling hawk feather? What do the aches of your body tell you? In the wild borderlands, bones are scattered across a trail, the desert wash drains nothing into nothingness, the darkness of night is impenetrable and we are alone with the ultimate fear. The story is written. Consider what it says to you.

Soul speaks in the borderlands. In tracking the fluid edge of dawn or twilight, of sea and horizon, you can read the signs. This is where stories are told and ancient language is understood. This is where your soul welcomes you home. The threshold waits for you.

Pause for a moment and reflect:

- Do you know how to ground yourself? How does it feel in your body to ground yourself?

- When was the first time you had a close connection with an animal or plant?

- What is your experience communicating with other-than-human animals, with plants, with Spirit? How do they respond to you?

- Is there a myth or story that has special meaning for you?

- Can you think of a time when you learned something from an animal or plant?

- What in your environment symbolizes the margins of the borderlands?

The Earth Walk

CHAPTER 7

The Earth Walk

LEAVING HOME IN THE dark for the earth walk, my arrival at the state park is timed for the edge of dawn. I make my way out of the parking lot and onto a path headed for the shoreline so I can work with the margins of sea and sky. I draw a line across the trail and step over into the borderlands.

The earth walk is a dawn-to-dusk ritual to help connect with soul and mystery. It brings the sacred into awareness. It is a way to work with the sacred horizons, the crossroads of dawn and dusk, earth and sky, water and rock, beginnings and endings. On the earth walk, one enters a sacred space with intention. Listen, look, pay attention. Consult with all beings that present themselves. Do this with the intention of encountering soul.

To make a beginning, an ending is needed. We begin by leaving the familiarity of the car and the road, leaving the asphalt parking lot, and leaving the trailhead. Leave behind certainty. Leave behind easy access to the last gas station's coffee and donuts, comfort and old ways of being. Leave behind the routine of meals and social engagements to enter into a fasting retreat. Leave it all behind for a new direction, for the hilltop and a new vision.

My earth walk story.

January. Beginning of day at Andrew Molera State Park in Big Sur. Rain! Rain and more rain! More than anything, I am exhausted. After a divorce, I fast-tracked graduate school and a job, internships, and learning the practice of therapy at a county mental health clinic for children. Some days are so heavy all I can do is come home and curl up on the couch with an old teddy bear, nursing grief and anger at the hardships children endure. At the same time, I am fighting a tumor and planning a surgery that will put an early and complete end to childbearing. I am stretched on the wheel of transformation, like it or not.

The river runs high; it is impassable. I sit on one bank of the river and look across at the unreachable opposite shore. The sea is rising and waves rush into the river mouth. The sky is dark and cloudy, the air misty with rain. Great trees, torn up by the roots, lie strewn about and are washed clean down to the bone.

The place feels raw and elemental. It is life ground down to core elements. It is primitive and primeval. The world is water, stone, and air. Fire has not yet come into the world. All is in movement, flux, transition, changing, grinding, and fluid. I find a smooth dark rock with a swirling white design that says even the stones once danced. It is the beginning, and the solid earth has not yet formed. The message is clear, there is power in beginnings and I will start my life from this raw core.

Instructions for the Earth Walk

Choose a place in nature that is comfortable to you. It should be wild enough not to have many human encounters or "improved" landscapes. Bring your practical knowledge of spending time alone in nature. Pay attention to the terrain, trail conditions, weather, animals, insects, and poisonous plants. Tell someone where you are going, when you expect to return, and arrange for a check-in when you have safely arrived home. Depending on where your earth walk will take place, you may want to be at a campsite the night before, and plan to stay over the following night. Begin your earth walk at dawn, at a time between first light and sunrise. Arrive at your place of beginning by dusk, when the sun has set but light remains in the sky.

Wear appropriate clothing for the terrain and weather. Take a daypack with water, extra clothing, a flashlight, and a small first aid kit. Even if you are planning to fast, take along emergency food in the event you find you must eat. A map is useful, even if you're in familiar territory, to plot out alternate routes and exits in case you need them. Take your journal and any creative supplies you want to use.

Ideally, this will be a dawn-to-dusk fast. Know your body and its needs, eat before you go out. If medically necessary, take a small food supply and any medication you require to keep yourself physically healthy. The purpose of the fast is to keep you from being distracted by eating activities and to bring on the benefits of awareness that come with fasting. Cultures around the world attest to the qualities of introspection gained when fasting. Do only what is safe for you.

Consider your intention, your questions, and what you need. Why have you come on this journey? What do you seek? Decide on a ritual to mark your entry across the threshold and into the borderlands. It can be as simple as drawing a line across the path with your foot, stating your intention, giving thanks and asking for protection. Then cross over.

Use any ritual of crossing the threshold that calls to you. You are entering sacred space. If you encounter people along the way, you can briefly acknowledge them, but do not stop and engage. Maintain an attitude of sacredness. Focus on how spirit speaks to you through all you encounter.

Notice where you are in order to return safely. Look all around and behind you as you walk. Notice how long it took to arrive at your present destination. The earth walk is a ceremony that requires attention to the world. There are strong currents, cliffs, heat, cold, and powerful forces large and small that require your attention. This is a contemplative walk, and not a time for extreme sports.

Orient yourself to the land. Notice the east, the south, the west, and the north. Arriving at dawn, you will see where the sun rises in the east. Opposite that is the west. Facing west, the south is on your left and the north is on your right. If orienting yourself in this way is new, bring a compass.

Consider the characteristics of the four directions. Walk in the direction that calls to you. Consider your questions and go in the direction that best symbolizes them. For example, if you are considering issues of health, you could walk in a southerly direction and consult with the south.

Walk and rest as you are called. Act as you are inspired – write, draw, dance, sing, meditate. Ask yourself where you are in your life journey, how you got there, where you will go next. Notice everything that speaks to you. Edit nothing. You may perceive thoughts, voices, impressions, visions, feelings. Listen to your gut. If an animal, plant, or other presence asks to be heard, listen to the message it brings you.

Return to your starting point by dusk. You do not want to be caught outside in the dark. Give thanks and re-cross the threshold into ordinary time. Then relax and break your fast, eat a meal. Fully reincorporate into ordinary reality. Drive only when you are grounded. Write your story.

The earth walk itself is a solitary journey. The full process of setting out and returning can also be done in partnership or with a group. You and any others can arrive at a meeting place, then each of you will go out in a separate direction. Return to meet together at the end. Participants should hold themselves in a sacred manner and avoid contact with each other when they are on the walk. After the ritual of return, the group can assemble, eat, rest, and chat. Then the group can meet in council and tell their stories.

Realistically evaluate your level of physical ability, outdoor experience and concern for any safety issues. If safety is a concern, you can hike out with a friend and together find a solo sit spot for each of you. Plan to stay in your sit spot and return to a designated meeting point at an agreed upon time. This way, each of you has seen where the other will be. Alternately, one person can provide field support for the person who is actually engaged in the ceremony, walking in together, and then leaving one person to sit in solitude. This method of staying in one place for the entire ritual is an ancient practice and well respected.

The Ceremony of Story

We are storytellers who create the stories of our lives every day. Return from your time on the land, join the circle and tell your story. Storytelling and the healing arts have been intertwined from the beginning of time. As we narrate our story, we tell ourselves and others who we are, we look for meaning and re-member the lost and fragmented parts of ourselves. Healing begins when we are witnessed. We are validated by another who listens with love. The listener has only to allow the story to rise up and affirm to the teller that they are seen and that *this* story is the gateway to creation.

The earth walk experience is individually inspired. There is no failure. If a person returns earlier than planned, it is still a valid experience. Sometimes the difficult journey is an unexpected invitation to descend into the sacred underworld or work with your shadow. It is as it must be. Use your skills for making deep inquiry and ask what this experience holds for you. Soul knows what is needed. Every journey is complete. There is an old story in which the Creator gives every living being a power: vision to Eagle, wisdom to Bear, swiftness to Horse. Little Sage in her dusty gray dress asks what power she could possibly have. The Creator responds, "Your power, little Sage, is to carry the prayers of the people." In the earth walk, some experiences will be inspired, some will be like ashes in the mouth, and some will be a puzzle. Every experience tells the story and every story is valuable. The storyteller is the only authority.

Night Walk

The night walk is similar to the day-long earth walk. Consulting with the night brings up a different vision. Choose a place where you feel safe. It is a good idea to go with a buddy, but head in different directions at a distance that allows for easy voice or light contact in an emergency. Plan a specific time to meet up, perhaps after two to four hours. Be familiar with the environment and terrain. Take a backpack with the essentials including a flashlight, although your journey should include as much darkness as possible. You can also travel to a place of introspection in the daylight, wait for sundown, and complete your ritual to sit with night.

Adaptation to Physical Needs

The earth walk can be modified, and these activities can be adapted for those who are not vigorous hikers. The basic elements described earlier can be modified based on physical or mental challenges.

Joan's Story

I guided a woman who, although she was just fifty, had difficulty walking due to hip pain and was planning on having hip surgery. In her younger years Joan was a robust, vigorous woman. She considered herself to be tough and street smart and she had survived a life of drug and alcohol addiction. We visited a coastal wildlife refuge with a handicap accessible trail. On an early weekday morning to avoid encountering other people, I accompanied her on a short walk to a sheltered bench in the windswept marine grasslands.

Joan completed the rituals for entering the borderlands and sat alone for about two hours while I waited out of sight, but near enough in case she needed help. Returning from her solo sit, she was moved to tears as she told her story. Having lived by her wits and toughness, with no one to show her tenderness, she was visited by the tiniest birds who told her that she was loved.

Pause for a moment and reflect:

- Where will you go for your earth walk? What is the terrain like? What flora and fauna does it have? What are the particular risk factors?

- Who is your check-in buddy and what is your arrangement?

- Have you gone through the day pack checklist? Do you have a map? Do you know how to use it?

- How do you feel in your body, mind and spirit? What is the safest way to complete your earth walk? Who will provide support?

- If you have any medical issues, have you consulted with your health advisors?

- How do you feel about your planned earth walk, what do you think about these feelings, what will you do, what ritual is appropriate? Work through the Four Directions with any concerns.

- What was your earth walk story?

Returning

CHAPTER 8

Returning

YOU RETURN HOME. Your house is waiting. Your partner asks how it was, your children cling to you, your dog pees in excitement, and your cat walks away. What now? What happened out there? It can be jarring to return from the Life/Death/Life dance in the Grand Cycle of Time and Space to find the checkbook doesn't balance.

Soon after greeting everyone, find time for yourself in the early or late hours of the day to sit quietly, meditate, and review what happened. Who did you encounter on your earth walk? What question was answered? What new vision did you return with? Clarify the message through contemplation, journaling, painting, or creating. Soul is there standing by and now you are in direct contact.

Return to the Wheel of Four Directions, described in Chapter 4, with your questions and deepen your understanding. For example, if you journeyed to the south to ask a question regarding your health and wellness, consider how you were answered. Follow the wheel to the west and contemplate how this affects your life. What roots were unearthed? Go to the north to discover what action can be taken to promote your health and healing. End in the east, what ritual could celebrate, commemorate, and give thanks for the gifts of soul? What will mark the endings and beginnings?

Complete this process again to answer questions about what to do with your vision. In the south, notice how it feels to have this vision. Go west to contemplate the meaning of this message in your life, its effect on those around you, what it means to bring it into the world. Go north to ask what actions you should take to realize your vision. What will you do? Turn east to create or enact a spiritual act of thanksgiving, of beginnings or endings.

Staying connected and nourishing the soul requires a conscious act. The relationship needs tending. Deepen the relationship and invite soul to settle in. Having gone into the wild to track soul, we know the skills -- stillness, listening, observation, attention. Anything that can bring back our attention is a good place to start. Create an altar at home. Any bookshelf, any ledge of a window, spot in your yard, or undisturbed space in your home can serve as an altar. Place items that remind you of your encounter with soul upon the altar – a feather, bit of stone or shell, candle, or anything that reminds you of the sacred.

Create a daily ritual. Simply salute the day as you go out the door. Greet your natural world relatives, the rosemary along the walkway, the trees in your yard, the sun, breeze, birds. A prayer can be made anywhere, anytime, in any language, in any manner that is sacred to you. Continue to journal and create. Return to your sit spot, make it a sacred place to you. Deepen the relationship. Get to know this as a soul home. Shamanic people will sometimes feed their power animal by wandering areas they know are important to it. Speak with soul in your sacred place and learn what nourishes it best.

Introduce friends and family to what you have experienced in nature. Children who create a nature journal or who are able to sit quietly and observe will learn about themselves, their world, and build useful life skills. In these times of electronic high adventure, being outdoors with the family is especially healthy and emotionally rewarding.

It is also possible that your earth walk journey has shown you that a part of your life needs to be let go, or needs to come to an end in order to move forward. This is not a path without challenges. Continue to work with the challenges, nourish soul, and stay engaged. The Japanese poet Basho wrote, "When my house burned down, I owned a better view of the rising moon."

We ask the question, "Who are my people?" We do not remain in the solitude of the earth walk. In following this path we can learn many lessons, and one is that we are in reciprocal relationship with the world. As you breathe out, your breath is inhaled by the oak, the chaparral, the grass. You drink water from deep aquifers filled by rain that seeps through pine needles and roots, rabbit bones, mushrooms, and the minerals of the Cretaceous period. Your blood runs with pine and rabbit and mushrooms and stone. None of us stands alone.

Pause for a moment and reflect:

- What is your vision? Take it through the wheel of Four Directions.

- How will you make space for the sacred in your life?

- What ritual would call up and renew your vision?

- Who are your people?

- What plant, animal, and earth relatives run through your blood and sinew? How are you related to the land?

The Web

CHAPTER 9

The Web

WHILE CAMPING IN THE Inyo Range, I woke up one morning to find a bright, sparkling network overhead. Spiderwebs covered with dew connected me to the trees, to my boots, and to the earth. Our inter-connection was clear. If I moved, the shimmering threads tugged the tree and broke the magic connection with the ground.

We all rely on each other. There is a "wood wide web," an underground network of roots that connect trees in a mutually beneficial life support system. The trees talk with each other through the mycorrhizal network of roots and fungi. Stronger plants send nutrients to younger or weaker plants. Those attacked by diseases or pests communicate this so neighboring trees can prepare to defend themselves.

As we acknowledge our relationships with our human and other-than-human neighbors, we create community. Develop these relationships. Nurture and celebrate them. Simple rituals of the day bring consciousness to our connections. Recognize your larger relationship with the natural world, and speak what you know to others.

Learn more about the land around you. A museum of natural history or park educational program can tell you about the features of your land, the watershed, geology, plants, animals, and early human inhabitants.

You may develop a special relationship with one of your wild neighbors and get to know your friend more intimately. Did you make a special connection with an animal or other being on your earth walk? Perhaps you encountered a special spirit, or you found kinship with a similar spirit in yourself. Acknowledge the spirit and honor the relationship.

As you go about the land, ask what it needs. What can you do that would be helpful? Perhaps trash can be collected. Communities often have beach cleanup days. Is there an effort to return native plants to the area or remove invasive species? There are groups that work to restore land to its native habitat. A neighborhood group in my coastal area walks across certain dunes to create gentle depressions in the sand that invite snowy plover nesting. Fishing groups work to protect waterways and help migrating fish survive.

We are all related. Oil well fracturing sites that pollute land and water sources are often located in poor, rural areas. Too often the people who bear the brunt of dangerous air and water quality or toxic waste are the poor and people of color. What does your relationship with water say to you? Environmental issues are social justice issues. Stand up and advocate for policies that serve the health of all people and the planet.

Many health-conscious people encourage farmer's markets and community gardens. In *Belonging: A Culture of Place,* bell hooks talks about the African American experience of "living deep in the earth." She writes of renewing this earth-based relationship. There are many possible allies who respect the relationship with the natural world.

Maybe what the land needs is a lighter touch from you and your family. Gandhi said, "Live simply so others may simply live." Re-evaluate your use of material goods, of energy, water, and other resources. Every day, science shows us how our way of living affects the planet at home and thousands of miles away. I recently learned that fleece fabrics release micro-plastics when they are washed. These micro-plastics are then ingested by zooplankton and then the entire food chain. How can we be more conscious of the quality and type of resources we use?

As you have been inspired by the land, inspire the land in return with your gifts. Make a spiritual gift of blessing. Bless the land and the water; bless the forest and the grasslands. Many people feel a spiritual presence at sites that have been used for ceremony and prayer. Add to the holy presence of your sit spot by making it sacred. We make so many connections. The redwood tree breathes out, we breathe in, and in-turn breathe out to the rest of the world. We share one breath, one "ruah," one spirit.

Pause for a moment and reflect:

- What is your relationship to the land? To the place where you live?

- Who are your allies?

- In what way will you support the land? What ceremony will bless the land?

Beginning

CHAPTER 10

Beginning

A PERSON SETS OUT on a quest for vision and healing. Driven by hunger, loneliness, and a half-remembered dream we seek a way home. "Going to the woods is going home," says John Muir. Heal the relationship and return home. Find solace in the waters and under stars. Sing home the salmon and lay down with the grass. Perhaps soul is seeking you while you yourself are seeking it. Does Mother Earth look for your face as you look for hers?

Many paths lead to vision, be they traditional religion, indigenous ceremony, scholarship, solitary contemplation, or the holy path of birth and family. I offer these stories as an old and a simple way of looking for personal meaning. Your own story will be different from mine but equally true. A wise woman once told me to "trust the ceremony."

Soul tracking, as with any practice, is a lifelong process. In youth, it is good to wander far and wide to learn what you are made of. A seventeen-year-old on a young adult rite of passage wrote, "Little did I know that there was a moment that would be a large part of what was meant for me in the journey: when I had to split from everyone to my campsite in an area I felt I belonged and needed to be, with only a tarp and a rope for a tent. There was a lot of waiting for a message which I was unknowingly in the process of getting. I didn't finally understand until we returned home." This youngster decided his lesson was about being on his own, finding his place, taking risks and coming to terms with the dark unknown. A good beginning for adulthood.

When lost in the mid-life chaos of existence, seek out the wild heart of the world for guidance. Often in the middle of a journey when I am tired and it is too wet and cold, or too hot, I ask myself, "What the heck are you doing?" And then it would happen that in the desert, looking at coyote scat on the dusty trail, I find myself looking at the holy Mother Earth, and then the dust is holy and the sacred surrounds me, and so maybe I contain the sacred too. Too much sun? Maybe just enough. Return to the wild again and again.

Deepen your practice. Get more "dirt time." Your spiritual tradition may offer an outdoor retreat. Those following a Native tradition may "go on the hill" for a vision fast. Ecotherapists and wilderness rites of passage guides can be found in most states. The National Outdoor Leadership School offers programs in wilderness skills and personal development. The School of Lost Borders has many offerings in nature-based rites of passage and soulful exploration on the land.

Ecology offers a model of lives interwoven. It is clear that each organism changes and is changed by the give-and-take of relationship. Finding ourselves in a relationship with the sacred earth we can be more deeply human. Can we extend our human compassion to our other-than-human relations? Is it possible to find compassion for the rocks and the water? If the root of the word "compassion" means "to suffer together," can we find it in us to "suffer together" with the planet?

Muir said, "Until he extends the circle of his compassion to all living things, man will not himself find peace." Once we know the open heart of nature, how can we reject the mutuality of the relationship? Go and make that relationship. Then give your vision life, bring the gift back. The people need vision.

The instructions for those who would be soul trackers: Listen. Be aware. Find true north. Know how to leave. Go out and track the edge of worlds. Return. Tell your Story.

Now Begin.

Appendix A

Checklist for a Day Hike

The best way to avoid forgetting things is to use a checklist. You can develop your own checklist. The following is recommended. Over time decide what works for you.

Day Pack with a belt
Hat or cap
Dark glasses
Shirt
Pants
Underwear
Walking shoes or boots
Socks
Whistle
Pencil
Notebook
Bandana – many uses
First Aid Kit
Electrolyte water or powder

Watch
Sunscreen
Lip balm
Insect repellent
Map
Compass
Toilet paper
Ziploc plastic bag
Knife
Water bottle
Windbreaker jacket
Raingear if needed
Emergency Food

Tarp and rope for rain or sun shelter if indicated.
Art supplies you may want to use.

First Aid Kit – Can be purchased from pharmacy or out-door store, should contain band aid, tape or moleskin for blisters, gauze, aspirin or other analgesic, soap for cleaning wound, needle/tweezer for splinter, personal medication.

Appendix B

Leave No Trace

The Leave No Trace Seven Principles

1. Plan Ahead and Prepare
2. Travel and Camp on Durable Surfaces
3. Dispose of Waste Properly
4. Leave What You Find
5. Minimize Campfire Impacts
6. Respect Wildlife
7. Be Considerate of Other Visitors

© 1999 by the Leave No Trace Center for Outdoor Ethics: www.LNT.org.

Plan Ahead and Prepare

- Know the regulations and special concerns for the area you'll visit.
- Prepare for extreme weather and emergencies.
- Schedule your trip to avoid times of high use.
- Use a map and compass to eliminate use of markings.

Travel and Camp on Durable Surfaces

- Durable surfaces include established trails and campsites, rock, gravel, dry grasses or snow.
- Protect riparian areas by camping at least 200 feet from lakes and streams.
- Good campsites are found, not made.
- Concentrate use on existing trails and campsites.
- Keep campsites small. Focus activity in areas where vegetation is absent.
- Avoid places where impacts are just beginning.

Dispose of Waste Properly

- Pack it in, pack it out. Inspect your campsite and rest areas for trash or spilled foods. Pack out all trash, leftover food and litter.
- Deposit solid human waste in catholes dug 6 to 8 inches deep, at least 200 feet from water, camp and trails. Cover and disguise the cathole when finished.
- Pack out toilet paper and hygiene products.
- To wash yourself or your dishes, carry water 200 feet away from streams or lakes and use small amounts of biodegradable soap. Scatter strained dishwater.

Leave What You Find

- Preserve the past: examine, but do not touch cultural or historic structures and artifacts.
- Leave rocks, plants and other natural objects as you find them.

- Avoid introducing or transporting non-native species.
- Do not build structures, furniture, or dig trenches.

Minimize Campfire Impacts

- Campfires can cause lasting impacts to the backcountry. Use a lightweight stove for cooking and enjoy a candle lantern for light.
- Where fires are permitted, use established fire rings, fire pans, or mound fires.
- Keep fires small. Only use sticks from the ground that can be broken by hand.
- Burn all wood and coals to ash, put out campfires completely, then scatter cool ashes.

Respect Wildlife

- Observe wildlife from a distance. Do not follow or approach them.
- Never feed animals. Feeding wildlife damages their health, alters natural behaviors, and exposes them to predators and other dangers.
- Protect wildlife and your food by storing rations and trash securely.
- Control pets at all times, or leave them at home.
- Avoid wildlife during sensitive times: mating, nesting, raising young, or winter.

Be Considerate of Other Visitors

- Respect other visitors.
- Be courteous. Yield to other users on the trail.
- Step to the downhill side of the trail when encountering pack stock.
- Let nature's sounds prevail. Avoid loud voices and noises.

Appendix C

Basic Outdoor Skills

READ THIS: *While many people enjoy hiking and other out-door activities, there is an inherent risk of injury or even death in any outdoor activity. Be realistic in assessing your skill level and physical ability. Consult with your physician concerning your medical issues. You may enjoy going on a group hike organized by an outdoor organization as a first adventure. The following information is based on the writer's experience and common practice. The information is by no means exhaustive, or the latest information. The reader should educate his or herself, consult with current experts and proceed at their own risk.*

Prevention

"An ounce of prevention is worth a pound of cure." Avoid getting too tired and dehydrated. Don't take unnecessary risks and be careful with your footing. Be prepared for the weather and protect yourself from sun exposure with a hat and sunscreen. Prevent foot blisters with well-fitting, worn-in footwear. If you begin to feel an irritated spot on your foot, stop and protect it with moleskin or tape before you get a blister. Drink only potable water. No matter how inviting and fresh the stream looks, these days it is not safe to drink untreated water.

Bad Weather

A little rain won't hurt. If there is a bad storm, seek shelter or turn back and try again another day. If there is lightning, stay away from high places, tall trees, other tall features, open places or wet marshy ground.

Hypothermia

Hypothermia is a serious drop in body temperature that ultimately can lead to death. It is usually caused by exposure to cold and wet, and aggravated by wind. Most hypothermia develops in temperatures of between 30 and 50 degrees. Prevent hypothermia by staying dry, and if wet, stay out of the wind and get warm. Some fabrics, such as wool, hold body heat better than other fabrics such as cotton. Severe shivering is an indication that you are at risk. Get into dry clothes, get warm and head back.

Fast Moving Water

The day hike proposed in this book does not require expedition skills. Stay safe and don't try a risky stream crossing. Moving water can be deceptive in speed, power and depth. Use common sense and take an alternate route.

Deserts

Prevent heat exhaustion by hydrating well; urine output should be clear and copious. Prevent dizziness and other symptoms of electrolyte imbalance and dehydration by bringing water containing electrolytes or by taking an electrolyte powder with you. Rest in the shade and avoid shrubby areas if you see rodent droppings in order to avoid disease like the hanta virus. Flash floods can occur, and six inches of fast water can knock people off their feet. Distant rain can create a flash flood in a wash, canyon or arroyo.

Stay aware of your environment and be able to get to high ground quickly.

Toileting

Use common sense. If you are on a day hike in a park, you can briefly come in from your hike and use the public toilets. If you cannot, then you may have to go off trail about 200 feet. Take note of features such as trees, rocks and shrubs as you head away from the trail and look back at where you came from. You can leave markers along the way, crossed sticks, rocks, keep looking back so you can return in the same way. Bury solid human waste. Make sure you are far away from water and drainage areas. Pack out paper and hygiene products. Some parks with high use require also that you carry out all human waste and may provide a bag for this purpose when you check in with the park service.

Lost

Take a map and hike on the trail. If you get a topographic map of the area, you will be able to see features of the land on the map that you can identify throughout your hike. Learn how to read a topographic map. Before you hit the trail, orient yourself to the four directions. Note the position of the sun. As you hike, look back at features of the landscape, note high points or other notable landmarks, know what direction you are heading towards and what direction you came from. At turns or switchbacks on the trail, look carefully at the pattern of wear on the trail and do not follow animal trails that may intersect with the hiking trail. If you think you may be lost, sit down and take a drink of water. Rest a minute and survey your surroundings and note the four directions, orient yourself. Prevent getting lost and hike in a manner fitting your experience, get used to the outdoors if the activity is new to you. You will, of course, have provided your check-in buddy with information on your trip. Park personnel and other hikers will likely cross your path if you are on a day hike. The universal whistle signal for distress is three short blasts, three long blasts, three short blasts, repeated. Stay hydrated, dry and comfortable.

Injury and Illness

Again, prevention is the best way to manage injury. Realistically assess your physical abilities. If you have medical issues, consult with your physician. If you plan to do a lot of hiking, prepare yourself by taking walks near your home. Studies indicate that the most common hiking injuries are blisters and injuries to ankle, shins and knees. Most falls occur from a misstep going downhill. Address the injury as best as you are able. Community organizations teach basic first aid classes. Rest, treat yourself with kindness, and return home if that is the wisest course of action. If you feel unwell, rest, return home and consult with your health advisor. With anything that seriously limits your mobility, stay on the trail, stay hydrated and get comfortable; of course, you will have made sure that your check-in buddy has all the information needed to rally a rescue.

Appendix D

Fasting

The dawn to dusk fast proposed in this book is not obligatory. The purpose of the fast is to reduce distraction and improve perception of inner and spiritual states. Fasts are commonly used for religious and spiritual purposes. Some cultures use the fast as a personal sacrifice in dedication to a greater purpose or to invoke the help of Spirit/Creator. Other cultures consider the fast as a healthful practice.

The basic recommended fast is to consume only drinking water for the period of the earth walk. If your medical condition requires you to eat during the period of the walk, then eat something very simple and no more than needed. Take regularly prescribed medication as indicated. Ask your doctor about this.

At minimum, the fast recommended is to abstain from recreational drugs, alcohol and tobacco, electronics, cell phones and similar entertainment, or food as entertainment for the period of the walk. Some cultures may use ceremonial plants that alter perception and are used with specific ceremony and support; the activities in this book are specific to a person's unaltered perception of self in the environment. The author discourages the use of any mind altering substances if you are following the activities in this book.

If you have never fasted before, try fasting at home first. Be aware of your physical and mental state when fasting, or at any time during the earth walk. It is normal to feel dizzy or a little weak. Practice awareness of self and the environment. Your earth walk can be to sit, rest and experience a deep inner journey.

If you find that you feel unwell and that it seems unwise to continue the fast, eat some of your emergency food and continue with your experience when you feel better.

The biggest adventure of the earth walk is within.

References and Suggested Reading

Abbey, Edward, *Desert Solitaire: A Season in the Wilderness*. New York: Ballantine Books, 1968.

Abram, David, *The Spell of the Sensuous: Perception and Language in a More-Than-Human World*. New York: Vintage Books, 1996.

Benson, Herbert, Klipper, Miriam Z., *The Relaxation Response*. New York: Avon Books, 1975.

Brown, Jr., Tom, *Tom Brown's Field Guide: Nature Observation and Tracking*. New York: Berkley Books, 1983.

Campbell, Joseph, *The Hero with a Thousand Faces*. New Jersey: Princeton University Press, 1973.

_____. *Transformations of Myth Through Time*. New York: Harper & Row, 1990.

Capra, Fritjof, *The Tao of Physics: An Exploration of the Parallels between Modern Physics and Eastern Mysticism*. Boston: Shambhala Publications, Inc., 1999.

Dhammarakkhita, V., *Metta Bhavana Loving-kindness Meditation*. Ampur Muang: Dhammaodaya Meditation Centre, 2001.

De Nevers, Greg, Edelman, Deborah Stanger, Merenlender, Adina, *The California Naturalist Handbook*. Berkeley: University of California Press, 2013.

Dillard, Annie, *Pilgrim at Tinker Creek*. New York: Harper Perennial, 1974.

Foster, Steven, with Little, Meredith, *The Four Shields: The Initiatory Seasons of Human Nature*. Big Pine: Lost Borders Press, 1998.

_____, *The Roaring of the Sacred River*. Big Pine: Lost Borders Press, 1989.

Gawain, Shakti, *Creative Visualization: Using the Power of Your Imagination to Create What You Want in Your Life*. Novato: The New World Library, 1978.

Hogue, Lawrence, *All the Wild and Lonely Places: Journeys in a Desert Landscape*. Washington DC: Island Press, 2000.

Hooks, bell, *Belonging: A Culture of Place*. New York: Routledge, 2009.

Houston, Jean, *The Search for the Beloved: Journeys in Mythology and Sacred Psychology*. Los Angeles: Jeremy P. Tarcher, Inc., 1987.

Johnson, Robert, *Inner Work: Using Dreams and Active Imagination for Personal Growth*. San Francisco: Harper & Row, 1986.

Kabat-Zinn, Jon, *Full Catastrophe Living: Using the Wisdom of your Body and Mind to Face Stress, Pain, and Illness*. New York: Bantam Doubleday Dell Publishing Group, Inc., 1990.

Kimmerer, Robin Wall, *Braiding Sweetgrass: Indigenous Wisdom, Scientific Knowledge, and the Teachings of Plants*. Minneapolis: Milkweed Editions, 2013.

Kornfield, Jack, *The Art of Forgiveness, Lovingkindness, and Peace*. New York: Bantam Books, 2002.

LeShan, Lawrence, *How to Meditate: A Guide to Self-Discovery*. New York: Bantam Books, 1974.

Muir, John, Cronon, William, *John Muir: Nature Writings: The Story of My Boyhood and Youth; My First Summer* in the Sierra; *The Mountains of California; Stickeen; Essays.* New York: The Library of America, 1997.

Niatum, Duane, ed., *Carriers of the Dream Wheel: Contemporary Native American Poetry.* San Francisco: Harper & Row, 1975.

Pinkola Estés, Clarissa, *Women Who Run With the Wolves: Myths and Stories of the Wild Woman Archetype.* New York: Ballantine Books, 1992.

Plotkin, Bill, *Soulcraft: Crossing into the Mysteries of Nature and Psyche.* Novato: New World Library, 2003.

Sheldon, Ian, *Animal Tracks of Northern California.* Auburn WA: Lone Pine Publishing, 1997.

Snyder, Gary, *Mountains and Rivers Without End.* Berkeley: Counterpoint, 1996.

_____, *Smokey the Bear Sutra.* "May be reproduced free forever," 1969.

White Bison, Inc., *The Red Road to Wellbriety: In the Native American Way.* Colorado Springs: White Bison, Inc., 2002.

Wilson, Edward O., and Kellert, Stephen R., ed., *The Biophilia Hypothesis.* Washington, DC: Island Press, 1993.

Winnett, Thomas, Finding, Melanie, *Backpacking Basics: Enjoying the Mountains with Family and Friends.* Berkeley: Wilderness Press, 1995

Resources

American Red Cross
www.redcross.org
Training in Basic Life Support and First Aid. Also sells books and supplies related to BLS and First Aid.

Benson-Henry Institute for Mind Body Medicine
www.massgeneral.org
Research and education for "Mind Body Medicine."

California Naturalist
www.calnat.ucanr.edu
Education "to foster a diverse community of naturalists and promote stewardship of California's natural resources through education and service." Citizen Naturalist programs are available around the country.

Center for Mindfulness in Medicine, Health Care, and Society
www.umassmed.edu
Research, training and services in Mindfulness Based Stress Reduction.

Daian Hennington, MSW
www.daianhennington.com
Ecotherapy and workshops in nature-based self exploration. Operating primarily on the California central coast.

Leave No Trace

www.lnt.org

Non-profit organization with a mission to protect the outdoors by "teaching and inspiring people to enjoy it responsibly." Developed the Leave No Trace Seven Principles.

National Outdoor Leadership School

www.nols.edu

International education and training in leadership and outdoor skills. Also a provider of the Wilderness First Responder, Wilderness Medicine and similar wilderness safety and rescue training programs.

School of Lost Borders

www.schooloflostborders.org

Since the 1970s, The School of Lost Borders "offers vision fasts and rites of passage training which cultivate self-trust, responsibility, and understanding about ones' unique place within society and the natural world." Headquarters at Big Pine, CA, programs worldwide.

Sierra Club

www.sierraclub.org

Environmental advocacy and education. Provides organized outings for every skill level. Outings and clubs are found around the world.

White Bison, Inc.

www.whitebison.org

American Indian/Alaska Native non-profit for recovery from addiction. Provides culturally relevant education through trainings and publications. "Our culture is prevention."

Wilderness Guides Council

www.wildernessguidescouncil.org

Membership organization for wilderness rites of passage guides, has a directory of guides who provide services in many states.

Index

ABOUT THE AUTHOR

Daian Hennington, MSW, is a guide into the borderlands of nature and psyche. A student of nature, culture and the spirit, she has studied with traditional, academic and other than two-legged teachers. She was initiated into her own wilder nature on a solo backpacking trip from Tahoe to Yosemite at the age of seventeen. As a practicing clinical social worker and ecotherapist, she has brought the healing benefits of nature into the clinical relationship for over two decades. Daian lives in the northern reaches of the Carmel River Watershed and offers workshops for self-exploration in the wildlands of California. Contact her at DaianHennington.com.

www.ingramcontent.com/pod-product-compliance
Lightning Source LLC
Chambersburg PA
CBHW030021290326
41934CB00005B/429